The Value of Money

$UBTRACTING COIN$ AND BILL$

PORTIA SUMMERS

Enslow Publishing
101 W. 23rd Street
Suite 240
New York, NY 10011
USA

enslow.com

WORDS TO KNOW

add–To count and make a total number.

bill–Paper money.

change–Money returned to as the balance of the amount paid.

currency–The kind of money a country uses.

dollar–The American currency.

subtract–To take away.

value–The worth of something.

whole number–A number that is complete and has no decimals.

CONTENTS

A QUICK LOOK AT MONEY

penny	nickel	dime	quarter	half-dollar	one-dollar coin
1¢	5¢	10¢	25¢	50¢	$1

one-dollar bill
$1

five-dollar bill
$5

ten-dollar bill
$10

twenty-dollar bill
$20

SUBTRACTING COINS

You have 3 nickels and a penny. How much money will you have left if you give away a nickel?

Start by counting the 3 nickels and the penny. These coins create a value of 16¢. Take 1 nickel away. How much is left?

You will have 11¢ left.

Another way to find the amount is to subtract.
2 nickels + 1 penny = 11¢.
10¢ + 1¢ = 11¢

Subtract the value of 1 nickel, 5¢. You subtract cents just like other numbers.

```
  11¢
- 5¢
───────
   6¢
```

You will have 6¢ left.

Moments in Minting

E Pluribus Unum is written on many US coins and bills. It means "one from many."

SUBTRACTING CENTS

You have 38¢ in your hand. You put 15¢ in your piggy bank. How many cents are left?
Do you need to know what kind of coins there are? NO!
You just need to know the value of the coins, which is 38¢ total.
Subtract to find your answer.

Start with the value of the money in your hand.
Subtract the amount that you put in your piggy bank.
38¢ – 15¢ = 23¢

You have 46¢. You give a quarter to a classmate. How much money do you have left?

What is the value of a quarter? 25¢. So, subtract.

46¢ – 25¢ = 21¢

Moments in Minting

The Bureau of Engraving and Printing uses 9.7 tons of ink per day.

SUBTRACTING BILLS

You had 2 ten-dollar bills and 2 one-dollar bills.
You spent 1 ten-dollar bill on a new T-shirt and 1
one-dollar bill on a soda.
How much money do you have left?

Start with the 2 ten-dollar bills and 2 one-dollar bills. Take away 1 ten-dollar bill and 1 one-dollar bill. Count what is left.

You could also solve this problem using subtraction.

First, find the amount you had.
2 ten-dollar bills + 2 one-dollar bills = $22.

Moments in Minting

A stack of one-dollar bills 1 mile (1.6 kilometers) long would value $14.5 million!

Then, find the amount you spent.
1 ten-dollar bill + 1 one-dollar bill = $11.
Subtract.
What you had – what you spent = what you have left.
$22 – $11 = $11

SUBTRACTING DOLLARS

How much is $58 minus $43?

The word "minus" means to subtract. Subtract dollars
just like you would other numbers.

$58 – $43 = $15

$58

– $43

= $15

CHANGE FROM COINS

An apple costs 33¢ at your school's cafeteria. You paid 35¢. How much change will you get back?

Change is the amount of money you get back when you pay for something with larger bills or coins than are needed. It is an important part of money math. Whenever you buy or sell something, you'll need to know about making change.

Find the change by subtracting the item's cost from the amount you paid for it.

35¢   –   33¢   = 2¢

A piece of candy costs 10¢. You paid with a quarter. What was your change?

A quarter is worth 25¢.

25¢   –   10¢   = 15¢

Fifteen cents can be made from a dime and a nickel or 3 nickels. What other combinations can you think of to make 15¢?

CHANGE FOR A DOLLAR

You used a one-dollar bill to pay for an eraser that costs 46¢. How much was your change?

A one-dollar bill is worth $1.00 or 100¢.
So:

$$100¢ - 46¢ = 54¢$$

Amount paid – cost = change

An ice-cream bar costs 85¢. You paid with a dollar bill. You got back two coins as change. What were the two coins?

Start with the amount you paid. One dollar equals 100¢. Subtract the cost of the ice-cream bar.
100¢ – 85¢ = 15¢

Your change was 15¢. What two coins together are worth 15¢?

A dime (10¢) and a nickel (5¢) together equal 15¢.

CHECK YOUR CHANGE

You spent 63¢ on a bookmark. You paid with a one-dollar bill. Your change was a quarter, a dime, and two pennies. Is this correct?

You can use addition to check your change. Add the value of your change.

Your change was a quarter, a dime, and two pennies.

25¢ + 10¢ + 2¢ = 37¢

Now, add the amount you spent and the value of your change.

63¢ + 37¢ = 100¢

100¢ = $1.00

Your change is correct.

You can also count to check your change.

Start with the amount you spent: 63¢.

Then use your change to count on, beginning with the least valuable coins.

Count one for each penny.

63¢   64¢   65¢

Count ten more for the dime.

65¢   75¢

Count twenty-five more for the quarter.

75¢   100¢

100¢ = $1.00 Your change is correct.

Moments in Minting

Most coins and bills have germs on them. Always wash your hands after handling money!

CHANGE FROM BILLS

A pizza costs $13.00. You paid for it with $15. How much was your change?

Find the amount of change by subtracting the cost of the pizza from the amount you paid.

$15 − $13 = $2

Amount you paid− cost = change

Your change was $2.00.

Living people cannot be featured on US currency. This dates back to revolutionary times. The Founding Fathers did not want to seem like many European monarchies that printed their kings on their money.

Moments in Minting

A book costs $12. You paid for it with a twenty-dollar bill. How much was your change?

Subtract the cost of the book from the amount you paid.

$20 - $12 = $8

Amount you paid – cost = change

What bills were your change?

A five-dollar bill and 3 one-dollar bills were your change.

You could also have gotten back 8 one-dollar bills.

LEARN MORE

BOOKS

American Education Publishing. *The Complete Book of Time and Money, Grades K-3*. Greensboro, NC: 2009.

Furgang, Kathy. *National Geographic Kids Everything Money: A Wealth of Facts, Photos, and Fun*. Washington, DC: National Geographic Children's Books, 2013.

WEBSITES

H.I.P. Pocket Change

www.usmint.gov/kids

The official website of the United States Mint

Science Kids

www.sciencekids.co.nz/sciencefacts/technology/money.html

Read fun facts about money.

INDEX

Published in 2017 by Enslow Publishing, LLC.
101 W. 23rd Street, Suite 240, New York, NY 10011

Copyright © 2017 by Enslow Publishing, LLC.
All rights reserved.

No part of this book may be reproduced by any means without
the written permission of the publisher.

Library of Congress Cataloging-in-Publication Data
Names: Summers, Portia.
Title: Subtracting coins and bills / Portia Summers.
Description: New York : Enslow Publishing, 2017 | Series: The
value of money | Includes index.
Identifiers: ISBN 9780766077201 (pbk.) | ISBN 9780766077218
(6 pack) | ISBN 9780766077225 (library bound)
Subjects: LCSH: Subtraction--Juvenile literature. | Money--
Juvenile literature.
Classification: LCC QA115.S855 2017 | DDC 513.2'12--dc23

Printed in Malaysia

To Our Readers: We have done our best to make sure all
website addresses in this book were active and appropriate
when we went to press. However, the author and the publisher
have no control over and assume no liability for the material
available on those websites or on any websites they may link
to. Any comments or suggestions can be sent by e-mail to
customerservice@enslow.com.

Portions of this book originally appeared in the book *I Can
Subtract Bills and Coins* by Rebecca Wingard-Nelson.

Photo Credits: Cover (green dollar sign background, used
throughout the book) Rachael Arnott/Shutterstock.com,
Fedorov Oleksiy/Shutterstock.com; (white dollar sign
background, used throughout the book) Golden Shrimp/
Shutterstock.com; VIGE.COM/Shutterstock.com (piggy bank
with dollar sign, used throughout book); Golden Shrimp/
Shutterstock.com (green cross pattern border, used throughout
book); p. 2 Heidi Meamber/iStockphoto.com; p. 3 Trong
Nguyen/Shutterstock.com; p.4 penny (used throughout
the book), mattesimages/Shutterstock.com; nickel (used
throughout the book), United States Mint image; dime and
quarter (used throughout the book), B Brown/Shutterstock.
com;half-dollar, Daniel D Malone/Shutterstock.com; one-
dollar coin, JordiDelgado/iStockphoto.com; one-dollar bill
(used throughout the book) Andrey Lobachev/Shutterstock.
com; five-dollar and twenty-dollar bills (used throuout the
book) Anton_Ivanov/Shutterstock.com; ten-dollar bill, Fablok/
Shutterstock.com; p. 5 RBFried/iStockphoto.com; p. 6 McIek/
Shutterstock.com; p. 7 Hill Street Studios/Blend Images/Getty
Images; p. 8 Zefart/Shutterstock.com; p. 9 Image Source/
iStockphoto.com; p. 10 Scott Eells/Bloomberg via Getty
Images; p. 12 :Inti St Clair/Blend Images/Getty Images; p. 13
Anna Hoychuk/Shutterstock.com; p. 14 Steve Debenport/E+/
Getty Images: p. 15 Leonard Zhukovsky/Shutterstock.com;
p. 17 junpinzon/Shutterstock.com; p. 19 Arvind Balaraman/
Shutterstock.com; p. 20 Peter Muller/Cultura/Getty Images; p
21. Velishchuk Yevhen/Shutterstock.com.